945.091
M

Mangione

Mussolini's march on Rome

W9-CHP-387

DATE DUE

JA 22			
OCT 21 '02			
FE 28 '95			
FEB 1			
FEB 2			
FEB 3			
FEB 4			
34-00			

MUSSOLINI'S MARCH ON ROME

Fascism, the system of government that was to scar the twentieth century, had its official beginning in Italy. On October 30, 1922, from all parts of Italy the Fascists gathered in a symbolic March on Rome. Benito Mussolini, invited by the king to form a government, arrived by train, wearing a frock coat and white spats. This ironic event marked the culmination of Mussolini's ambitious political ascent and the beginning of a political and social phenomenon that would have worldwide repercussions.

PRINCIPAL CHARACTERS

BENITO MUSSOLINI, founder and head of the Fascist Party

VICTOR EMMANUEL III, King of Italy

LUIGI FACTA, Prime Minister of Italy on the eve of the March

EMILIO DE BONO, Chief of the Fascist Militia and oldest member of the Quadrumvirate, which was in charge of the March

ITALO BALBO, Fascist extremist, youngest member of the Quadrumvirate

MICHELE BIANCHI, Secretary-General of the Fascist Party, member of the Quadrumvirate

CESARE MARIA DE VECCHI, war hero, promonarchist member of the Quadrumvirate

DINO GRANDI, high-ranking member of the Fascist Party, who questioned the wisdom of the proposed March on Rome

GABRIELE D'ANNUNZIO, famous Italian author and an early exponent of Fascism who created much of its mystique

MUSSOLINI'S MARCH ON ROME

OCTOBER 30,1922
A dictator in the making
achieves political power in Italy

By Jerre Mangione

A World Focus Book

FRANKLIN WATTS, INC.
NEW YORK, 1975

The author wishes to thank Dr. Jack E. Reece
of the Department of History of the University
of Pennsylvania for his valuable criticism.

Picture credits: Keystone pp. ii, 31, 34A&B; Library
of Congress pp. 3, 5, 43, 56, 58; United Press International pp. 9, 18B, 52; Hulton Picture Library pp.
23A, 24, 32, 57; Giraudon p. 18A; Italian Cultural
Institute pp. 23B, 38, 39, 40, 48; Wide World
Photos p. 55.

Cover by Nick Krenitsky

Library of Congress Cataloging in Publication Data

Mangione, Jerre Gerlando, 1909–
    Mussolini's march on Rome.

    (A World focus book)
    SUMMARY: Traces Mussolini's life and the
events leading up to his rise to power in Italy during the 1920's.
    Bibliography: p.
    1. Mussolini, Benito, 1883–1945—Juvenile lit-
erature. 2. Italy—History—1914–1945—Juvenile literature. [1. Mussolini, Benito, 1883–1945. 2. Dic-
tators. 3. Italy—History—1914–1945] I. Title.
DG575.M8M27   945.091′092′4 [B] [92]   74–9816
ISBN 0–531–02782–1

Contents

Fascist Finale

An excited crowd was gathering at an abandoned gas station off Milan's Piazzale Loreto, eager to see the corpses on display. The date was April 29, 1945. A few hours earlier the Italian Partisans had executed Benito Mussolini, who had been dictator of Italy for more than twenty-three years. They had found him two days earlier dressed in a German uniform, trying to escape into Switzerland. In addition to Mussolini, the Partisans had executed his mistress Claretta Petacci and four high Fascist officials. They had brought the corpses to the Piazzale Loreto because it was here that the German army had executed fifteen Italian hostages the year before.

While a few armed Partisans tried to hold back the crowd, men and women jumped up and down, trying to get a better view of the corpses and reviling the dead with their obscenities and curses. Two young men got to Mussolini's body and savagely kicked it in the face. Others fired shots into the corpses. A woman with a revolver pumped five bullets into Mussolini's corpse, one for each of her sons who had been killed in World War II. Unable to control the crowd, the Partisans summoned a fire truck that turned a hose on it. But the crowd held fast. Some of them were furious that they could not see the corpses.

"We demand to see them," they shouted. "We have a right to see them." The Partisans hesitated, not knowing what to do. Then the strongest of them began to hold up each corpse by its armpits above his head. "Higher, higher," the crowd yelled. "We can't see them." A voice roared, "String them up," and the crowd took up the cry.

A half hour later the six corpses, each with its ankles tied together, were hanging upside down from the steel girders of the gas station, about six feet from the ground. Mussolini and Claretta Petacci were placed in the center of the grisly spectacle. The former dictator was dressed in his black Fascist uniform, boots and all, his face the color of putty. There was dirt and blood on the girl's face but its beauty was still discernible. The crowd jeered when a woman

1

stood on a box to adjust Claretta Petacci's skirt, which had become undone. A man poked her body with a stick, and for a moment it swayed and twirled like that of a marionette, its arms extended as though pleading for compassion.

But compassion for Fascists was hardly the mood of the Italians, especially in Milan where Mussolini had supervised the birth of Fascism in March, 1919, and where in October, 1922, he had waited nervously for his March on Rome to materialize. The anger of the crowd watching the six corpses in that abandoned gas station reflected the bitterness of the Italian defeat in World War II. The war, which was the direct outcome of Mussolini's dictatorship, wiped out the promises and dreams of the Duce, who for two decades had been telling the Italians that under his leadership Italy would achieve the prestige of a great world power. Five years of the war had brought devastation to the nation, leaving it a physical wreck with deep moral scars. Perhaps the deepest scar came from the Italians' realization that they had permitted themselves to be ruled by a dictator who put his personal sense of glory above that of the nation's welfare.

To understand how Fascism came to Italy, one must examine the events that led up to the March on Rome, the incident in which Mussolini took over power in Italy, as well as the background of the man who led the March and who was mainly responsible for replacing the democratic structure of the Italian state with a powerful dictatorship that was to change the course of world history. It was Mussolini's dictatorship that served as a model for Adolf Hitler and his henchmen.

Problem Child

Benito Mussolini was born on July 29, 1883, in a big iron bedstead fashioned by his blacksmith father. His father, Alessandro, who was

Alessandro Mussolini.

a socialist, christened him after the Mexican revolutionary general, Benito Juarez, who sixteen years earlier had spearheaded a violent revolution against Emperor Maximilian. For the first three years of his life young Benito, who was later to become a forceful and eloquent orator, refused to talk. "It will pass," a doctor assured his parents. And he added prophetically, "I have the feeling that when the time comes he may even talk too much."

The Mussolini family lived in three crowded rooms of a tumble-down building in Predappio, a small town in Romagna, one of the most impoverished regions in central Italy. Benito's mother, Rosa, was a schoolteacher, the only one in the village, but her pay was small, and her husband's earnings as a blacksmith did not amount to much. To make matters worse, Alessandro was inclined to be careless with money. Except for his wife's ability to be thrifty, the family would have often gone hungry.

Although Benito's parents loved each other, they had little in common. Rosa was a devout Catholic who kept a portrait of the Virgin Mary above their bed. Alessandro, an atheist and a passionate revolutionary, had no use for Catholicism. At his insistence, a portrait of his hero, Giuseppe Garibaldi, hung next to that of the Virgin Mary. Alessandro not only talked of revolution but also behaved as a revolutionist. Before his marriage, he had spent six months in jail for his left-wing activities. He had never attended school but he was well read, particularly in the literature of revolutionists, and even wrote articles for several socialist journals.

Rosa Mussolini would have liked Benito, her firstborn, to become a priest, but it soon became clear that the boy was drawn to the philosophy of his father. "Socialism," Alessandro would tell his son, "is open and violent rebellion against our inhuman state of things. It is justice coming to an unjust world, a free pact among men." Rosa insisted that Benito and his brother and sister attend mass, but Benito seldom remained until the end of the services, claiming that the smell of incense made him feel sick.

4

Rosa Mussolini.

Only a mother could have imagined young Mussolini as a priest. He was bad-tempered, obstinate, and disobedient, constantly getting into scrapes and coming home with his face scratched and bleeding. As a boy, he liked to display his contempt for authority by stealing and vandalizing. He also enjoyed playing the role of leader. Once he led a gang of boys on a looting expedition to a quince orchard. When the farmer saw the children stealing his quinces, he seized a shotgun and fired at them. While trying to escape, one of the boys fell and broke his leg. Except for Benito, the others ran to safety, leaving their comrade behind. Benito faced the farmer defiantly, then lifted the boy to his shoulder and carried him out of the orchard.

Yet he was a dreamer as well as a fighter and when he wasn't scrapping with his schoolmates, he would spend hours by himself, studying nature and the birds, and reading. "I shall astonish the world some day," he told his mother. His father had no doubt that Benito would, but his mother worried about his inability to get along with others and his lack of discipline. When Benito was nine years old, she persuaded her husband to send him to a boarding school some twenty miles away which was operated by the Salesian Fathers. His mother hoped that the strict discipline of the priests would make Benito more subdued.

Before delivering Benito to the Salesian Institute, his father told him, "Pay attention to what they teach you, especially the geography and history—but don't let them stuff your head with nonsense about God and the saints." Benito replied that he need have no worry on that score. "I know there's no such person as God," he added.

For Benito the next two years were filled with bitterness and trouble. He hated almost everything about the boarding school—his schoolmates as well as the priests. He had a special dislike for the rich schoolboys who sat at a separate table and were served better food than the rest of the students. In his second year there he stabbed a schoolmate in the buttocks with his penknife, and he was expelled.

Next his parents enrolled him at a school a few miles from their home. But Benito went on behaving as though rules and regulations were not intended for him. As usual, he was always spoiling for a scrap. While fighting with a schoolmate, who had pushed his arm as he was writing, Benito again pulled out his penknife and stabbed the boy. Again he was expelled. Yet though his conduct was intolerable to his teachers, they admitted that he was an unusually intelligent student, and he was readmitted to the school as a day student. Three years later, at the age of eighteen, he passed his final examinations and was awarded a teaching diploma.

A Radical in the Making

For his first teaching job young Mussolini traveled to the township of Gualtieri, one hundred miles away from his parents' home. But, as might be expected, the local gentry did not approve of his unconventional behavior and his argumentative nature, and his appointment was not renewed. At that point he decided to heed his father's advice to "go out into the world and take your place in the great fight." Telegraphing his parents for enough money to buy a train ticket to Switzerland, he set out to join "the great fight" with only a couple of francs in his pocket.

For the first time Mussolini went hungry. Sleeping in a packing crate under a bridge and begging for food, he was arrested as a vagabond, just before his nineteenth birthday, and put in jail. In Geneva he was again arrested when, in a fit of hunger, he "attacked" two Englishwomen sitting on a bench eating their lunch. "I could not restrain myself," he wrote. "I threw myself on one of the old witches and grabbed the food from her hands. If they had made the slightest resistance I would have strangled them—strangled them, mind you!"

In Lausanne he was lucky enough to meet a group of kindly Italian socialists who fed him and helped him find employment. His dislike for ordinary work kept him from holding any of his jobs long enough to learn a trade. But his Italian friends were impressed with his education and his eloquence and, after he had been in Switzerland four months, they elected him secretary of an association of bricklayers and manual laborers. The job afforded him an opportunity to develop his talent as an orator. Speaking at demonstrations and strike meetings, young Mussolini discovered what he had suspected all along—that with his speech and gestures he could electrify an audience.

In a debate with a minister on religion, the young orator announced that if God existed, he would give Him "five minutes to strike me dead." When he was still alive at the end of that time, the audience cheered him wildly. His romantic appearance—the glittering dark eyes in the tormented scowling face—and his fierce gestures appealed to audiences. And Mussolini thrived on their response. The excited applause of audiences became a tonic which the future dictator of Italy was to require the rest of his life.

During this same period in Switzerland Mussolini also began to achieve a reputation as a radical journalist who never hesitated to express his contempt for the military, the Church, and the monarchy. In blunt language he described the kings of Europe as "intellectual nonentities" and declared that "their mentality is barely sufficient to sign decrees." Lashing out against all armies, he recommended desertion as the "only infallible method" of destroying them. He reserved his most acid opinions for religion. At the age of twenty-one he published a sixty-page pamphlet, *Man and Divinity,* in which he wrote that "religion in science is an absurdity, in practice an immorality, in men a disease."

*Benito Mussolini, at the
age of twenty-one when he was
a socialist in Switzerland.*

8

Later, when Mussolini became dictator of the Italian people, his actions as the head of the state completely contradicted these opinions, for he not only collaborated with the Italian monarchy and the Vatican, but he also transformed Italy into a militaristic power with expansionist ambitions. In those early years of Mussolini's career only a few of the radicals who knew him sensed that he was more ambitious for himself than he was for the socialist causes that he championed in such violent language.

Angelica Balabanoff, a Russian socialist who became an intimate friend of Mussolini when he was a young radical, became aware that behind his revolutionary facade he was timid and unsure of himself. She also understood that his socialist ideals were not based so much on his love for the working class as they were on his yearning for fame and leadership.

Living Dangerously

Even as a young revolutionary Mussolini sometimes surprised his socialist friends with actions that were inconsistent with what he preached. His speeches against military establishments, for example, urged soldiers to desert; he himself was an army deserter, having failed to do his stint in the Italian army. Yet when the king of Italy, as a gesture to celebrate the birth of his son, declared an amnesty for army deserters, Mussolini left Switzerland and became a soldier in the Italian army, shocking some of his socialist friends. As a soldier, he behaved properly and received an honorable discharge.

Yet almost as soon as he was released from the army, he became a rebel again and a frequent contributor to socialist journals. At the age of twenty-five he went to Trento, which was then part of Austria, to work with a trade union and write for a left-wing newspaper. Unfortunately for Mussolini, the Trento police had been warned by

Swiss officials that he was "a violent and impulsive" radical. The Austrian police did everything possible to make life miserable for Mussolini. In the space of less than eight months he was jailed six times; the newspaper he was editing was banned eleven times. Finally, he was ordered to leave the country for attempting "to incite violence against the authorities."

On returning to Italy Mussolini joined his father who, now in poor health, had given up his trade as a blacksmith and was operating a wine shop. Since the death of his wife four years before, Alessandro had been living with a mistress who was the mother of five children. The youngest of her daughters was a pretty girl of sixteen called Rachele. Mussolini had fallen in love with her oldest sister, Augusta, but when she turned him down to marry a man she considered more stable, a gravedigger by trade, he decided he would marry Rachele. When her mother and his father objected to the marriage, Mussolini produced a pistol and threatened to shoot himself if he did not have his way.

Mussolini took Rachele as his wife in orthodox socialist style— without benefit of clergy. The couple lived in two damp and sorry rooms; they could barely manage on the small salary Mussolini earned as secretary of the Socialist Federation in Forlì. Some of his earnings supported a newspaper he founded—a four-page weekly called *La Lotta Di Classe* (The Class Struggle) which he wrote in its entirety. When the couple's first child, Edda, was born, Mussolini celebrated the event by spending half of his week's wages on a cradle.

Although the young revolutionary devoted a great deal of his time to writing and reading—he was particularly fond of writers like Friedrich Nietzsche and Georges Sorel who advocated the use of social violence for social change—he considered himself a man of action. When the price of milk was raised in Forlì, Mussolini, backed by a shouting mob, pushed his way into the mayor's office and issued this ultimatum: "Either the price of milk is lowered or I'll advise these people to throw you and all your staff over the balcony." The price of milk was reduced.

To live dangerously, to create violent situations that would express his revolutionary ardor, became the basic tenets of Mussolini's creed. In 1911 when Italy sent troops into Tripoli, he lost no time trying to stir up the opposition of the people of Forlì. The Italian government was claiming that it had sent troops to protect the property of its Italian subjects. But, as Mussolini pointed out in his newspaper, the real purpose of the military expedition was to acquire Tripoli and the rest of Libya for itself. "Before conquering Tripoli, let the Italians conquer Italy," Mussolini fumed in an editorial. "Bring water to parched Puglia [one of Italy's poorest areas], justice to the South, and education everywhere. On to the streets for the General Strike."

The nationwide strike had been called by the General Confederation of Labor to protest the military adventure in Tripoli. The strike turned out to be a fiasco in most of Italy, but not in Forlì. Mussolini joined forces with Pietro Nenni, then a young political idealist, in transforming the local strike into a militant action against the war. Led by the two young men, the workers in Forlì armed themselves with pickaxes and, in an effort to stop troop trains, began tearing up railroad tracks. They were dispersed by a contingent of cavalry that attacked with drawn swords. But a little later, responding to Mussolini's fervent oratory, the workers regrouped and forced all business and industry in the city to come to a standstill.

Although martial law soon brought an end to the two-day strike and the arrest of its two leaders, Mussolini regarded the episode as a glorious revolutionary event. At his trial, where he acted as his own lawyer, Mussolini told the judges, "If you acquit me, you will give me pleasure. If you condemn me, you will do me honor." He was sent to prison again, this time for five months.

A Socialist's
Rise and Fall

Mussolini's reputation as a socialist firebrand was rapidly spreading beyond the boundaries of Romagna, and he made the most of it. At the next National Congress of the Socialist Party, he launched a furious and brilliant attack on four socialist deputies who represented the conservative wing of the party. Mussolini accused them of compromising with the establishment. The party, he insisted, must get rid of all such dross. Swayed by his oratory, the party expelled all four deputies, and Mussolini was made a member of the party's executive committee.

That wasn't all. A few weeks later the executive committee, now dominated by left-wing socialists, unanimously selected Mussolini as director of the party's official newspaper *Avanti*, a post which he had long coveted. Exhilarated by these triumphs, Mussolini moved to Milan, where the newspaper was published, leaving his family behind in Forlì. For his deputy editor he chose Angelica Balabanoff, the Russian socialist who had befriended him in Switzerland, but let his staff know that he would write all the editorials and political articles. *Avanti* then had a circulation of 28,000. Within a few months Mussolini's flair for dramatic journalism began to pay off. The circulation doubled and it kept on increasing until, two years later, it had reached the 100,000 mark.

As *Avanti's* circulation and influence grew, so did Mussolini's popularity as the "Duce" (leader) of Italian socialism. But suddenly a great war broke out in Europe which was to produce a drastic change in his career. On July 28, 1914, following by a month the assassination of the Crown Prince of Austria and his wife in Sarajevo, Austria declared war on Serbia. Within a few days the major European powers were at war with one another. In Italy it was feared that the Triple Alliance—a secret treaty with Germany and Austria made in 1882—might drag the Italians into a war against Great Britain, France, and Russia.

Mussolini, who had previously denounced the secret treaty, now began to denounce all the nations participating in the war. He demanded that the Italian government maintain a policy of "rigid neutrality." The headlines in *Avanti* roared with such slogans as "Down With War," "Down with Arms and Up with Humanity," and his fellow socialists enthusiastically endorsed his stand. Yet at the same time Mussolini, like many other Italians, was beginning to have second thoughts about the desirability of maintaining a neutral position. While few Italians were willing to enter the war on the side of Germany and Austria, there was a strong movement to intervene on the side of England and France, with whom the Italians felt a closer bond.

"The defeat of France would be a death blow to liberty in Europe," Mussolini told a fellow journalist. "The Socialist Party should not turn its back on the possibility of intervention in favor of France." Yet *Avanti* kept attacking the possibility of intervention. "Francophilism threatens to make common cause with the warmongers," Mussolini wrote in an editorial. "No, a thousand times no. We must be neutrals as proletarians, neutrals as Italians."

In Milan rumors began to circulate that Mussolini must be a man of two minds. What he wrote in *Avanti* was clearly contradicted by the opinions he was expressing to friends and acquaintances. Several newspapers urged him to stop being a "Hamlet Mussolini" and to let Italians know what he truly believed. Following their advice, he wrote a long prointervention statement which he published in *Avanti* in the name of the Socialist Party without consulting any of its members. The article, which appeared on the same day that Mussolini attended a meeting of Socialist Party executives in Bologna, outlined the political advantages of going to war against Austria and concluded with the opinion that absolute neutrality was a dangerous and harmful policy. Italians, he added, enjoyed "the privilege of living in the most tragic hour in the history of the world," and he asked:

14

Did the socialists want to be "inert spectators of this grandiose drama" or did they want to be part of it?

The article shocked his fellow socialists not only because it contradicted the neutrality stand Mussolini had been promoting so vigorously but also because it was printed without explaining that the opinions expressed were his own and not those of the Socialist Party. Infuriated by their hostile reaction, he resigned his editorship of *Avanti,* and then began to worry about how he was going to support his family. But he didn't have to worry long. In less than a month he began a newspaper of his own, *Il Popolo D'Italia,* financed by a publisher who advocated intervention on the side of France.

The first issue of the newspaper printed on its masthead two mottoes that bristled with martial fervor: "He who has steel has bread" and "Revolution is an idea which has found bayonets." In a signed editorial on the front page Mussolini proclaimed that "today antiwar propaganda is cowardice" and called on "the young in years and the young in spirit" to go to war. "It is a word which in normal times I would never have used, but which today I am compelled to utter loudly in sincere good faith, the fearful and fascinating word— War."

Ten days later at a meeting of socialists, called especially to decide Mussolini's fate, he tried to explain why he was now working for a cause that he had recently been attacking. He was hissed and booed and called a traitor and a Judas, and could barely make himself heard above the angry uproar. *Chi paga?*—Who is paying you?—the socialists shouted, convinced that he had been bought off. *Chi paga?* There were rumors (later proven to be true) that in addition to the financing provided by the interventionist publisher, Mussolini was receiving money from the French government which, of course, was anxious to have Italy enter the war as France's ally. Mussolini denied the charges but no one was in the mood to listen to anything he said. They jeered and cursed him and pelted him with coins and spitballs.

"I gather from this assembly that my fate is sealed," Mussolini managed to say.

"Yes. Down with the renegade," was the cry.

"Today you hate me because you will love me," Mussolini shouted. "Twelve years of my life in the party should be a sufficient guarantee of my socialist faith."

But no one, not even his friend Angelica Balabanoff, believed him, and he was formally expelled from the ranks of the Socialist Party. "I am ousted but not tamed," he wrote in the next issue of his newspaper. "If they consider me dead, they will have the terrible surprise of finding me alive, implacable, obstinately resolved to fight them with all my forces."

Italy Enters the War

The interventionists were then a minority in Italy—most Italians preferred to stay out of the war completely—but with Mussolini and the writer Gabriele D'Annunzio, leading the campaign for going to war against Austria and Germany, more and more Italians began rallying to their cause. The circulation of Mussolini's newspaper skyrocketed. "Every time that blockhead Mussolini writes an article the circulation goes up," a newsvendor told Rachele who, incognito, was checking sales of the newspaper in Milan.

Refusing to recognize that Italy was poorly prepared for war and that its economy was still suffering from its military adventure in Tripoli, Mussolini and his followers campaigned aggressively for intervention. But their efforts would have counted for nothing had it not been for Prime Minister Antonio Salandra and other key government officials. They pushed for intervention, believing that the war would be a short one and would bring Italy territories that would add to her economic and geographic strength. Although the interventionists remained a minority, they finally got their way. On April 26, 1915, Italy and the Allies signed the secret Treaty of London which promised Italy certain border territories at the end of the war. On May

24, a few weeks after the Italians had renounced their old treaty with Austria and Germany, Italy was at war with Austria.

In order to counteract the indifference and hostility of the many Italians who had opposed intervention, the Italian government invited the nation's most eloquent patriot, the writer Gabriele D'Annunzio, to sound the call to arms. An even greater actor than Mussolini, D'Annunzio rose to the occasion with an inflammatory speech in which he addressed himself to "the young in spirit" and to an Italy "which shall be greater by conquest, purchasing territory not in shame but by blood and glory."

Among the "young in spirit" who promptly volunteered was D'Annunzio himself. The Archangel Gabriel, as some of his admirers called him, was small and frail and fifty-two years old, but like Nietzsche he believed in living dangerously—the same idea which was to motivate so many of the Fascists. Mussolini, more cautious about endangering his life, did not enlist but waited until he was drafted. In a few months he was back in army uniform, and remained on active duty for seventeen months, five of which were spent in the front-line trenches. Although he was a conscientious soldier, he was in no way outstanding and did not rise above the rank of corporal. Just as he was about to be promoted to the rank of sergeant, he was wounded during a practice-firing session when a shell exploded inside a cannon. Five men near Mussolini were instantly killed. He was thrown a distance of fifteen feet with forty-four fragments of shrapnel in various parts of his body.

Within a month Mussolini underwent twenty-seven operations, most of them without an anesthetic in order to forestall the possibility of gangrene. When he returned to the offices of *Il Popolo D'Italia* he was on crutches, and, according to his enemies, he continued using the crutches longer than was necessary. One of his first actions was to resume his fierce attacks on the socialists, who were still officially opposed to the war. When the badly equipped Italian army suffered a major defeat at Caporetto, Mussolini blamed it on the actions of the socialists, the pacifists, and the neutralists.

The left-wing firebrand who used to shout "Down with War and up with Humanity" now initiated a "Stand to the Finish" campaign. As part of it, he urged the Italian government to suppress publication of the socialist newspapers and to declare martial law in those northern cities where antiwar groups were strongest. At the same time, with an eye on a political career, he presented himself as a champion of the working classes, assuring his readers that although he was no longer a socialist, he was antibourgeois and anticapitalist. For the first time he began to write about the advantage of having a dictator govern Italy, "a man who is ruthless and energetic enough to make a clean sweep." A little later he broadly hinted that he himself could qualify for that role. The idea of a March on Rome was beginning to take root.

Postwar Havoc

The end of the war on November 11, 1918, was celebrated as a great Italian triumph from the Alps to Sicily, but as the results of the war became clear, the mood of celebration changed to that of disillusion. Six hundred thousand Italians had been killed in the fighting; more than a million and a half soldiers had been wounded. Because of this tremendous sacrifice the Italians felt cheated when the Versailles Peace Conference did not grant them all the territories that had been promised in the Treaty of London. To add to their bitterness, the war had left their country in a deplorable economic condition.

Some three million returning veterans, many of them young men without a trade, needed jobs desperately. Yet employment was scarce, and the cost of living was continually rising. During the war the

Left: Gabriele D'Annunzio, a portrait by Romaine done in 1912.
Right: Mussolini in 1917 in the uniform of a
bersagliere, a member of a crack corps of the Italian army.

Italian government had promised that returning soldiers would be given land. But the landowners were unwilling to cooperate, and the government was doing nothing about keeping its promise. As a result, ex-soldiers in several rural districts invaded the large estates and took possession of land that was not in cultivation.

Conditions in the towns were even worse. The industrialists and merchants who had profited from the war continued to make excessive profits, while many families in the towns were in danger of going without food. Shops were looted and there were battles with the police. Mussolini, always eager to win popular support, wrote in his newspaper: "Down with the oppressors of the poor!"

Although peace had come, the feeling against the war was stronger than it had ever been. Returning soldiers were often attacked without any provocation. In Milan the situation became so bad that the army decreed that officers on leave should wear only mufti "to avoid inflaming the population." The unhappiest of the war veterans were demobilized officers, who numbered about ten thousand, and a dangerous group of ex-soldiers known as *Arditi*. These were the daredevils of the Italian army who had been in the front lines of battle. Wearing black hats adorned with skulls and bones and carrying daggers between their teeth and a grenade in each hand, the *Arditi* (the Italian word for "daring") had become famous for their ability to strike terror into the ranks of the enemy.

During the war these "Black Flames," as they were also known, had been regarded as heroes and accorded many special privileges whenever they were on leave. Now they found it difficult to settle down to peacetime. Restless and eager for action, they created so much trouble that the military command considered dissolving their group. Mussolini, sensing the possibility of putting their recklessness and courage to his own use, let it be known that he was their friend. At a war victory celebration attended by some *Arditi* dressed in their all-black military uniforms, Mussolini addressed them as "fellow soldiers" and said:

"I defended you when the Philistine was defaming you. I feel some of myself in you, and perhaps you recognize yourselves in me. You represent the admirable, warlike youth of Italy. The flash of your knives and the roar of your grenades will wreak justice on all the wretches who want to hinder the advance of the greater Italy. You shall defend her! We shall defend her together!"

The next day a committee of *Arditi* visited Mussolini at his newspaper office to present him with their flag: a black banner with a white skull. Mussolini accepted it with thanks and hung it on a wall behind his desk. The presentation marked the inception of the Fascist Blackshirts, the ruthless followers of Mussolini who, after their March on Rome, would impose a right-wing dictatorship on the nation.

Birth of Fascism

The *Arditi* had another staunch friend in Gabriele D'Annunzio, Italy's superpatriot, who in September of 1919 made dramatic use of their services. Disgusted by the refusal of the Versailles Peace Conference to give Italy cities and territories which Italians felt rightfully belonged to them, D'Annunzio declared he would save Italy from the "humiliation" of the "mutilated victory" imposed on her by her former allies. He organized a band of *Arditi* and two battalions of ex-soldiers, and marched on Fiume, one of the cities claimed by the Italians. In defiance of all the governments who had designated Fiume as a free city, D'Annunzio and his men took possession of it in the name of the Italian government without firing a single shot.

Although the seizure of Fiume created an international sensation, the Italian government and the other nations chose to ignore it, perhaps in the belief that D'Annunzio and his followers would soon tire of the occupation and leave. But for fifteen months they showed no signs of tiring, and actually increased in number. D'Annunzio's bold action thrilled many Italians, particularly right-wingers, and a number of them rushed off to Fiume to join their hero. Always the showman, the diminutive poet made the most of the situation. He gave himself the title of *Comandante* of Fiume, and harangued the citizens of the city and his followers daily, and sometimes with as many as four speeches a day.

To keep his audiences in high spirits, D'Annunzio taught them the Roman salute and conducted dialogues with them. He would ask, "To whom Fiume?" and the crowd would shout back, "To us!" The crowd would also repeat war cries which D'Annunzio invented. Eventually he would bring the dialogue to a close by shouting, "You with me, I with you, always." These techniques for exciting audiences were later adopted by the Fascists and used at their big rallies.

As *Comandante,* D'Annunzio proclaimed a new constitution for Fiume and threatened a march on Rome with himself at the head of it. Mussolini may well have been jealous of all the publicity D'Annunzio's escapade was receiving, but in his newspaper he supported the action and even declared that from now on Fiume should be regarded as the capital of Italy. Yet D'Annunzio did not feel that Mussolini was doing enough for his cause, and wrote him a letter filled with bitter complaints. "You go on babbling, while we fight," he scolded. "You do not even help us with a fund drive . . . Wake up! and be ashamed of yourselves." Mussolini, who could not afford to antagonize D'Annunzio, promptly launched, through his newspaper, a money-raising campaign to help maintain the occupation of Fiume. Later on, it was discovered that Mussolini retained some of the funds to use for his own political activities.

Even before D'Annunzio's occupation of Fiume, Mussolini realized that the *Arditi* and other discontented ex-soldiers could be developed into a significant source of political power. On March 23, 1919, a rainy Sunday morning, he met with one hundred of them in a small hall in Milan and founded the first Fascist contingent, *Fasci di Combattimento.* The word *Fasci,* which signified an ancient symbol

Above: an Italian demonstration over the Fiume question.
Below: D'Annunzio with his troops outside of Fiume.

Mussolini and D'Annunzio.

of the Roman Empire, literally meant a bundle of elm rods and an axe bound together with a red cord. It symbolized the powers of life and death that Roman consuls had over their subjects. Mussolini and the newly organized Fascists clasped hands over a dagger and swore: "We will defend Italy, ready to kill or die."

The first Fascist effort to gain political power was a failure. In November, 1919, when Mussolini was one of the Fascist Party candidates for a seat in Parliament, the Blackshirts were badly defeated. Out of 270,000 votes cast in Milan, the birthplace of the Fascist Party, only 4,657 went to Fascist candidates. The socialists, on the other hand, scored heavily, capturing 156 of the 535 seats in Parliament.

The day after the election the jubilant socialists printed a mock obituary of Mussolini in *Avanti:* "This morning a dead body in a state of decomposition was fished out of the Naviglio [Milan's main canal]. It would seem to be the body of Benito Mussolini." On the same day a parade of socialist workers symbolically carried a coffin past Mussolini's residence. These insults infuriated Mussolini and his followers, and they struck back. While the socialists were staging a celebration rally that evening, a hand grenade, such as that associated with the *Arditi,* was tossed into the crowd, and many were wounded. When the police searched Mussolini's office, they found a small arsenal of bombs and explosives: the filing cases were stuffed with them. Mussolini was charged with "armed plotting against the State" and jailed.

He was released shortly afterwards, but it was one of the lowest points in Mussolini's career. Some of his closest associates left him; his newspaper began losing circulation and money. In his bitterness, he talked of giving up his career as a journalist, but went on writing articles in which he savagely attacked his enemies, waiting for a change of luck.

He was not obliged to wait long. Unemployment and inflation were creating serious problems which the Italian government could not control. Strikes and riots were daily occurrences. Public buildings were attacked by mobs. As the situation worsened, the position of the

Fascists grew stronger. Split internally by warring factions of extremists and moderates, the large Socialist Party was unable to exert any effective leadership. The weakness of the socialist position, coupled with the chaotic conditions of the nation, provided Mussolini and his Fascist squads with the opportunity to develop into a powerful political force.

"The Bolshevik Menace"

At first there were only a few branches of the new Fascist Party, most of them in the northern cities of Italy where Mussolini was well known. By the end of 1920 fewer than 20,000 Italians had enrolled as members. But by the time the March on Rome was staged two years later, the number of Fascist Party branches had increased to 2,200. These were mainly in northern and central Italy; only a few existed in the south, only one in Sicily. Altogether, they represented an enrollment of 320,000 members who regarded Mussolini as their Duce.

Much of the money needed to finance Fascist groups came from industrialists and other capitalists who were afraid that Italy's chaotic postwar economic condition would enable the nation's powerful left-wing forces to seize government power. The fear that there might be a "Bolshevik" takeover of the government was triggered in September, 1920, when 600,000 metal workers seized a number of factories in various parts of Italy and flew the red flag above their chimneys. Italians who had a vested interest in the establishment blamed the situation on "The Bolshevik Menace," referring to the revolution that the Russian Bolshevik Party had successfully staged in their country three years before.

Actually, there was no danger of a left-wing seizure of government power. Although there were some communists and socialists who claimed that a revolution was the only solution to Italy's problems, most of the left-wingers either believed that a revolution would come about by itself or insisted that all changes in the system of government be made through legislative action. The occupation of the factories by metal workers lasted only a month. During the negotiations between the unions and the industrialists, Mussolini supported the demands of the workers. After the factories were returned to their owners, he scoffed at the fears of those who had talked of a left-wing takeover of the government. "To say that there is still the danger of Bolshevism in Italy," he wrote in his newspaper, "is to allow fear to prevail over truth. Bolshevism is over and done with."

While negotiating with the metal workers' unions, the Italian government was also trying to deal with D'Annunzio for a peaceful resolution of the Fiume situation. But D'Annunzio refused to take part in any negotiations, declaring he would rather die than surrender. Determined to settle the issue, the government dispatched a naval division and an army corps to the besieged city. It took only two shells fired from the battleship *Andrea Doria* to persuade D'Annunzio that he would rather surrender than die.

Strategy of Terror

With no political party able to direct the nation's business, Mussolini sensed that Italy was ripe for a drastic change of government. Although he had admitted there was no danger of a Bolshevik takeover, he now initiated a new Fascist strategy that was based on the widespread fear of Bolshevism. Instead of attacking the socialists from the left, as he had been doing, he now began to attack them from the right as a reactionary, calling them dangerous revolutionaries. His attacks included the Christian Democrats and anyone else who expressed dissatisfaction with the establishment. With the support of the middle classes and the industrialists, he and his Fascist squads launched a violent anti-Bolshevik campaign throughout all of Italy.

Deliberately, the Fascist squads created the atmosphere of a civil war. In the name of law and order, they killed, burned, and pillaged. Any Italian who belonged to a union or cooperative or who was suspected of being a left-winger was considered a fit target for their violence. Encouraged and financed by industrialists and large landowners, who were frightened into believing that a Bolshevik revolution which would deprive them of their properties was imminent, the Fascist squads often had the cooperation of the police as they plundered and murdered. Imitating the style of the *Arditi,* they wore black shirts and sang patriotic songs as they beat up or murdered their victims, and looted and burned down union headquarters. They referred to such acts of violence as "punitive expeditions."

Although the Fascists were a minority political group, far outnumbered by several other political parties, they were tightly organized and highly effective, able to assert their power in a variety of ways. In many towns where the local governing councils consisted of left-wingers and Christian Democrats, the Fascists offered them the alternative of resigning or being murdered. Their actions were not always politically obvious. In Florence the Fascists ordered food stores to cut their prices by 20 percent. If a store refused to comply, the Fascists destroyed its stock. In Alessandria they assembled all of the local pickpockets and swindlers and presented them with the choice of signing up in the Fascist Party and going straight or being beaten up.

One of the favorite "persuaders" of the Fascists, which was first used during D'Annunzio's occupation of Fiume, was castor oil. Before forcing it down the throats of their victims, the Fascists sometimes added benzine to the oil. Another "persuader" was a nineteen-inch bludgeon known as the *manganello*. It is not surprising that the favorite Fascist slogan was *Me Ne Frego* (I don't give a damn).

Claiming to be the saviors of Italy, the only group capable of rescuing the country from Bolshevism, the Fascists murdered some 3,000 anti-Fascists between October, 1920, when they launched their bloody crusade, and October, 1922, when the March on Rome took place. The Fascist loss of life during this period was considerably lower, 300, one-tenth of the anti-Fascists murdered. In the same period the Fascists also destroyed 17 newspaper and printing presses, 59 cooperative apartments, and 110 trade union halls.

The more terror the Fascists spread, the more Italians joined their ranks. Many did so out of fear of being beaten or murdered. Others joined with the hope of gaining some personal advantage, among them landlords, industrialists, peasants, and ex-soldiers. The landlords hoped the Fascist gangs could protect their properties. The industrialists hoped they would break the back of the trade union movement. The peasants hoped the Fascists would help them acquire some land of their own. Ex-soldiers expected to gain respect and employment. Fascist membership included opportunists of all kinds who hoped to better their economic and social status. Even a few distinguished artists and intellectuals—such as Arturo Toscanini and Benedetto Croce—favored the Fascist movement at first, although later, when they became aware of its destructive qualities, they turned anti-Fascist.

Despite such support, the Fascists could not have achieved the power they did without the assistance of such government officials as Prime Minister Giovanni Giolitti and the members of his cabinet. Giolitti disliked the Fascists, but he and his cabinet decided to strengthen their hand and in that way diminish the strength of the socialist and Christian Democratic members of Parliament, never dreaming that their tactic would pave the way for a Fascist dictatorship. Giolitti began his political maneuver by allowing thirty-five Fascist deputies (Mussolini among them) to be elected as members of his National Block. He also permitted army generals to equip Fascist squads with rifles and trucks. At the same time, law enforcement agencies as well as magistrates were tacitly encouraged to disregard any disturbances initiated by the Fascists, and to intervene only when they could be of service to them. To help provide the Fascists with the mobility they needed, the government also gave many of them free railroad passes.

The Rise of
the Blackshirts

At the age of thirty-seven Mussolini had become a national figure, the head of a political party whose size and might were growing rapidly. Yet he was not as confident of his ability to seize power as some of his followers were. At Fascist meetings he often spoke of the urgency of staging a coup d'état to overthrow Parliament and put the Fascists into power. But privately he was not at all certain that the Italian people would support such an action. He was afraid that in the public mind violence was being equated with the Fascist image and that before long there would be a strong reaction to their campaign of terror and violence. With this in mind, Mussolini signed a "pacification treaty" with the socialists. But three months later he abandoned it when he learned that some of his staunchest Fascist followers, who were far more militant than he, had no intention of abiding by the treaty.

More and more Mussolini found himself obliged to give in to the militancy of the Fascist leaders around him. When they proposed that the Fascists seize three cities as a demonstration of their political and military strength, he offered no serious objections. All three actions were to be dress rehearsals for the March on Rome. The march on Ravenna came first. Led by Italo Balbo, a handsome twenty-five-year-old ex-soldier who was the most radical of the Fascist leaders, 300 Blackshirts, some of whom had marched sixty miles, took possession of Ravenna in September, 1921, without any bloodshed. Ferrara, a city to the north of Ravenna, was taken the following May. While Balbo held its prefect at gunpoint, 63,000 Fascists seized all the key points in the city. Less than three weeks later the Blackshirts again demonstrated that they could capture and hold a city. This time they marched into Bologna, where for five days 20,000 Blackshirts were in complete command.

*Mussolini about the time when
he was starting the Fascist Party.*

Not all of Mussolini's right-hand men were extremists like Balbo. Dino Grandi, who was one of his most devoted disciples, did not believe that a March on Rome was necessary. He argued that the Fascists had achieved enough political muscle to win control of the government by legitimate means—that is, through elections—"without resorting to the extreme means of an heroic but dangerous insurrection." An insurrection, he feared, would alienate a good many Italians who had been won over to the Blackshirt cause. Why take that risk? he asked.

Although Grandi's opinion was not shared by most of the other Fascist leaders, Mussolini recognized its merit and tried to negotiate with various officials for a larger Fascist representation in the government. When his efforts proved unsuccessful, he began to listen more closely to the extremists who were confident that, with the government increasingly weak, the Fascists could stage an effective coup d'état. As proof of its weakness they could cite the fact that in three years Italy had had four prime ministers. They could also point out that although the nation was beginning to gain economically, the government appeared unable to cope with the strife that the Fascists were creating.

When the socialists called a general strike in August, 1922, to protest the violence and disorders initiated by the Fascist *squadristi*, Mussolini delivered a tough ultimatum to the prime minister: Either the government should take steps to break the strike or his Fascists would do so. As soon as it became apparent that the government was not taking any action, Mussolini carried out his threat. Taking advantage of the public's exasperation with the strikers, the Fascists, in the name of law and order, burned more than 100 socialist head-

Italo Balbo, in a photo taken sometime in the mid thirties.
He was the most radical of the Fascists.

quarters to the ground. In Milan they destroyed the printing presses of *Avanti.* Their actions were not entirely destructive. In some cities, they won the gratitude of the citizenry by operating trains and trolleys, which the strike had brought to a halt, and allowing people to travel on them free of charge.

As soon as the general strike collapsed, Mussolini took a harder line. "The March on Rome has begun," he declared on August 11. A week later, he announced, "The century of Democracy is over." Early in October his newspaper published the military regulations for a Fascist militia, an act that was patently illegal since it created a Fascist army outside the regular Italian army. Such an action should have resulted in the arrest and imprisonment of Mussolini and his staff, but the authorities did nothing. The prime minister then was Luigi Facta, an honest but weak individual who was optimistic to an absurd degree. Instead of ordering Mussolini arrested, Facta foolishly adopted a wait-and-see attitude, trusting that everything would eventually turn out for the best.

The Quadrumvirate

Three weeks later, on October 24, the Fascists held a big rally in Naples. There Mussolini thrilled his followers with the bluntness of his stand. He told the huge assembly, "Either the government will be given to us or we shall seize it by marching on Rome."

"Roma, Roma," shouted his friends in the audience. "Roma, Roma," thousands of others echoed.

When Gabriele D'Annunzio heard of the proposed March, he

Above: Dino Grandi, in a 1936 photo. Grandi favored more legitimate approaches to power than the March represented. Below: during the general strike in Milan the Fascists took over the streetcars and ran them as free transportation.

could not contain his antagonism toward Mussolini. "Rome, Rome," he was said to have cried, "will you give yourself to a butcher?" Still the most popular figure in Italy, the poet had intended to stage his own march on Rome. It was the second time he felt betrayed by Mussolini. The first betrayal took place when Mussolini had not raised his voice in protest over the government's action in chasing D'Annunzio and his legionnaires out of Fiume. D'Annunzio had provided the original inspiration for the Fascist movement and much of its mystique. But it was clear that Mussolini was through with him now, anxious that he remain in the background.

Of late D'Annunzio had irked Mussolini by promoting the idea of replacing the diminutive King Victor Emmanuel III with the king's cousin, the Duke of Aosta, who was a much more attractive personage as well as a war hero. Although the duke was a Fascist sympathizer, Mussolini opposed the idea. He had no love for any monarch and would have preferred an Italian government without royalty, but since the promonarch sentiment among his followers was too strong to ignore, he favored retaining the present king.

In his speech at the Fascist rally in Naples he spoke favorably about the House of Savoy, leaving no doubt in anyone's mind that he would have no part of the Aosta branch of the royal family. As a shrewd politician, Mussolini realized that if King Victor Emmanuel could be assured that his position would not be disturbed when the Fascists tried to seize power, he would be more inclined to accept a Fascist rule.

Mussolini's day in Naples was a busy one. After his speech, he inspected 6,000 members of the newly formed Fascist Militia. In the evening he met secretly with the four highest-ranking members of the Fascist Party, the Quadrumvirate as they called themselves. They were to direct the March on Rome. The youngest of the four was Italo Balbo; he was also the most daring. One historian said of him: "The sight of blood, of buildings set on fire by his Fascist squads, the perpetration of violence, elated him as no drug could have done." The oldest member of the Quadrumvirate was General Emilio De

Bono, a small man with white beard and moustache who had served in World War I. His willingness to command the Fascist Militia, even while still a member of the regular army, shocked Italian military men; but since the Italian army was considered friendly to the Fascist movement, no action was ever taken against him.

The third member of the Quadrumvirate was Cesare Maria De Vecchi, a Fascist deputy who was a year younger than Mussolini. He had won six decorations for his heroism in the war and had been promoted to the rank of captain. De Vecchi was a conservative who was deeply devoted to the House of Savoy. The political brain of the Quadrumvirate was Michele Bianchi, Secretary-General of the Fascist Party, who had worked closely with Mussolini during the rise of Fascism. He was the same age as Mussolini and, like the Duce, had been a newspaperman and one of the founding fathers of the Fascist movement.

De Vecchi and Balbo were the chief activists of the Quadrumvirate, the ones who prodded Mussolini whenever he seemed overly cautious. At one point, when Mussolini hesitated to commit himself to a March on Rome, these two men convinced him that the Blackshirts would march on Rome whether Mussolini was with them or not. Balbo, the most aggressive of the leaders, may have understood Mussolini's strengths and weaknesses better than any other member of the Quadrumvirate.

On the podium Mussolini invariably impressed his audiences as self-confident, a born commander, the essence of virility and courage. But that was mainly because he was an actor. Without an enthusiastic audience responding to his words and gestures, he became a lonely and vacillating personality. A socialist who had once

Over left: Emilio De Bono, a Fascist leader who had been a general in the regular army.
Over right: Cesare De Vecchi, an activist Fascist who had been a hero in the First World War.

known him well described him as "a rabbit, a phenomenal rabbit that roars." He added, "People who see him and do not know him mistake him for a lion." Balbo had more respect for Mussolini than that, yet he realized that his usefulness to the Fascists was based not so much on his personal qualities as on the popular myth that he was endowed with the extraordinary powers of a superman.

Prologue to
the March

At its secret meeting with Mussolini the Quadrumvirate selected October 28 as the date for the March on Rome. General De Bono argued that four days of preparation would not be enough, and recommended that the march be postponed for six months. But he was outvoted by the others, who felt that the element of surprise would be more likely to act in their favor than months of preparation. Leaving it up to the Quadrumvirate to plan the details of the March, Mussolini returned to Milan on October 26.

The next day the Quadrumvirate issued a general proclamation addressed to all Fascists and Italians announcing that "the hour of decisive battle has come," and that the army of the Blackshirts was about to march on Rome in order to restore its ancient glory. The proclamation warned the Italian army and the police not to interfere, since the Fascists were not marching against them but against "a political class of half-wits and idiots that in four long years have not been able to give a true government to our nation." The proclamation added, "We shall be generous toward unarmed adversaries, but inexorable with others."

Michele Bianchi, Secretary-General of the
Fascist Party and its leading political strategist.

Although Mussolini had led the Quadrumvirate to believe that he was completely in favor of the March, his actions belied that. As soon as he returned to Milan, he worried that the March might be a failure and bring an end to the Fascist movement. Once again he began negotiating with government leaders in the hope of winning enough concessions from them to make the March unnecessary. He had reason to worry. If the army were to oppose the marchers, the Blackshirts could be stopped without any difficulty. More important to him than the March itself was the *threat* of the March. How skillfully he manipulated that threat would determine whether or not he could use it as an instrument for seizing control of the government.

Some historians believe that Mussolini's negotiations in Milan with intermediaries of the prime minister were intended to provide a smokescreen for the Fascist mobilization that had just begun to take place. Yet Mussolini's efforts seemed genuine enough as he tried to persuade Prime Minister Facta that the March on Rome could be averted by simply giving the Fascists several cabinet positions, including the Ministry of War. Luckily for Mussolini, as it turned out, Facta could not decide what to do.

The rumors about the impending March had generated a great deal of anxiety among members of Parliament, but the prime minister seemed temperamentally incapable of initiating any action that would put a stop to the affair. Always the optimist, he could not believe that a few thousand men would dare march on a city that was protected by troops and artillery. A number of suggestions for squelching the enterprise were made to him. A former minister tried to persuade him to organize a countermarch as a means of stopping the Fascists, but got nowhere. A parliamentary deputy, who was well versed in law, was certain that arresting Mussolini "would finish the business."

Luigi Facta, Prime Minister of
Italy before and during the March.

Facta expressed astonishment. "How could we possibly arrest him?" he asked the deputy.

"Just give the order to any police chief," the deputy replied. But he was not taken seriously.

The prime minister finally came up with an idea of his own. It was based on the intense feeling of rivalry that was known to exist between Mussolini and D'Annunzio. Facta's plan was to exploit this feeling by inviting all the disabled veterans of World War I to Rome on November 4, Italian Armistice Day, under the leadership of D'Annunzio. The prime minister was confident that the patriotic fervor generated by such an occasion would make Mussolini's attempt at a coup d'état impossible. D'Annunzio readily accepted the invitation to lead and to address the disabled veterans, and sat down to prepare his speech. But there was a basic flaw in the plan: the prime minister's mistaken assumption that the March on Rome would be staged on Armistice Day.

The Fascists Mobilize

The top leadership of the Fascist Party knew that the secret date of the March was October 28, but withheld it from the Fascist ranks. There was great confusion as to when it was supposed to take place. On October 26 the Naples office of *Il Popolo D'Italia* unsuccessfully tried to reach Mussolini in Milan to ask whether there was any truth to the rumor that the March would start that night. Partly to avoid making any decisions and partly to add to the confusion as to when the March was scheduled, Mussolini kept away from his office and made certain he was seen in public by going to the theater that evening.

At the same time, his friend Bianchi was in Rome talking to newspapermen about the several cabinet resignations that had just been submitted to the prime minister. "The only possible solution of the crisis is to entrust the succession of Facta's cabinet to the Honorable Mussolini," he told the press. "The party which has determined the crisis is the Fascist Party; it is therefore the head of that party who must be called on to form the new cabinet." He added that the Fascists represented the political sentiment of the nation. "The day before yesterday there could be talks of coalition directed by other top men with our collaboration. But today the situation is radically changed."

Afraid that Mussolini might be willing to settle for something less than the post of prime minister, Bianchi telephoned him. His hunch proved to be accurate. Mussolini had been offered four ministries in the new cabinet and was obviously tempted. Bianchi told him that it was no longer the moment for discussing such offers. "What is going to happen is as fated as Destiny itself." When Mussolini agreed with that, Bianchi asked if he could quote him, but this time he hedged. "Before you do . . . Let's try to talk again tomorrow," Mussolini said.

But mobilization of the Fascists was already under way. The Fascist command in Perugia, impatient with waiting, had given the order to proceed with the master plan for the March. The Fascists began seizing public buildings, railroad stations, and army depots. They were also cutting telephone lines and requisitioning trucks and guns. Partly because of Mussolini's apparent state of indecision, the Quadrumvirate was not functioning as a single body. Bianchi was in Rome keeping close watch on the political developments. De Vecchi was busy with members of the royal court trying to win them over to Mussolini's demands. Balbo was traveling from one city to another trying to coordinate the actions of the mobilized Fascists.

Although not a regular member of the Quadrumvirate, Dino Grandi was in Rome working behind the scenes, trying to arrive at a political solution for the Fascists that would give them control of the government without the use of force. In this effort he had the help of De Vecchi, who, like Grandi, was a parliamentary deputy and had access to key members of the government, including the king. As a result of their maneuvers, Mussolini was offered the opportunity of participating in the formation of a new cabinet in which Antonio Salandra, a right-wing former prime minister who had the sanction of the king, would serve as president and Mussolini as minister of the interior. Mussolini, either because he sensed the possibility of a complete triumph or because he was surrounded by Fascists who would not have tolerated his acceptance of any compromise offer, turned down the proposal. "Victory should not be mutilated by last-minute concessions," he wrote in his newspaper, adding that "the government must be decidedly Fascist."

In the meantime, Fascists in every part of the country were trying to enact the master plan for the March. It consisted of five parts: 1) mobilization and occupation of public buildings in all principal cities, 2) a concentration of Blackshirts at Perugia and at four different towns near Rome, 3) the delivery of an ultimatum to Prime Minister Facta for the general stoppage of government control, 4) the seizure of all ministries, 5) the establishment of a Fascist government. It was a carefully devised plan, but it was lacking in two important aspects: direction and equipment.

De Bono, the only member of the Quadrumvirate left at Perugia, was out of touch with his associates. In the field the Fascists were badly equipped and inadequately armed. Most of the would-be marchers were without conventional weapons. Those who were armed did not have enough ammunition; some had none at all. There were only a few machine guns among the four columns of Fascists that were to converge on Rome. Nowhere among them was a single heavy gun that could attack the 30,000 soldiers of the regular army stationed in the capital. Food was generally in very short supply, and some of the men were so hungry that they threatened mutiny.

To make matters worse, a heavy rain began to fall all over Italy. At Monterotondo, one of the main concentration points, the thermometer registered nine degrees above zero. The commander in charge there wrote in his diary: "Not a lira to hire cars . . . Our men are soaked to the skin and have eaten nothing since yesterday." At Santa Marinella, another concentration point, a Fascist officer noted in his journal: "Needs: water, food, money. It is impossible to keep in touch with the High Command in Perugia."

In Milan Mussolini was in the barricaded building of *Il Popolo D'Italia,* which was guarded by seventy members of the Fascist Militia. The news he was receiving was not encouraging. As soon as the Italian cabinet learned that the Fascists were mobilizing, it voted to impose martial law on the entire country. Announcements to that effect were posted in Rome and telephoned around the nation. Orders were issued for the arrest of all Fascist leaders.

Rome was ominously quiet. Every strategic point in the city— the king's palace, the government buildings, the railway stations, electric generating stations, postal and telegraph offices—were surrounded by army troops equipped with field guns, machine guns, and armored cars. The army officers in charge were confident that a few rounds of ammunition would destroy any Fascist attempt to capture the city. In other parts of the country, the army began blowing up railroad tracks in order to hinder the movement of the Fascists.

The King's Dilemma

In the meantime, a tense drama involving King Victor Emmanuel and Prime Minister Facta was unfolding in the Palazzo del Quirinale. It was a crucial time—the night before the Fascists were to march on Rome. The king, annoyed that he had been summoned from his vacation in Tuscany where he had been hunting in the pine woods, was faced with a decision that he dreaded. Martial law had already been declared but the proclamation required the king's signature to be valid. The cabinet, which had drawn up the proclamation, had taken it for granted that the king would sign it and had publicized it throughout the land.

Now the king seemed reluctant to sign the document. He had

no love for the Fascists but he dreaded the possibility of a civil war and unnecessary bloodshed. There were other considerations that weighed heavily on his conscience. Five army generals had already declared themselves Fascists and were participating in the March. Generalissimo Diaz, head of the Italian army, had already expressed friendly feelings for the Blackshirts. When the king telephoned the general that night to determine how the army would react when confronted with a March on Rome, Diaz replied, "Your Majesty, the army will do its duty—but it would be better not to put them to the test."

The king may also have been influenced by his mother, Queen Margherita, who was favorably disposed toward the Fascist cause. Nine days before she had secretly met with two members of the Quadrumvirate—De Vecchi and General De Bono—and extended to them her best wishes for their cause. "I know your plans have only one end," she added, "the safety and glory of our country." She had considerable influence on the king and, in this instance, she took care to use it. Not only was she impressed with Mussolini and his movement but also she knew that if her son did not cooperate with him, he might be compelled to abdicate or, at the very least, lose his throne to his cousin the Duke of Aosta.

While the king was trying to decide what to do, Prime Minister Facta, optimistic as always, remarked that he was still hopeful of reaching an "amicable compromise" with the Fascists. The king grabbed at this straw. Since there was such a possibility, why, he asked, should he sign the martial law decree? He instructed Facta to return the decree to the cabinet for reconsideration. Facta was shocked. Like the other members of the cabinet, he had assumed the king would sign it. He had never known the king to refuse to sign a document submitted to him by the cabinet.

The cabinet deliberated all night. Then, led by Giovanni Amendola, a young statesman who was to be badly beaten up by the

Victor Emmanuel III, King of Italy.

Fascist secret police three years later, it voted to stick to its original decision. Again the king refused to sign the decree. "The only thing it can accomplish is civil war," he said. He placed the document in a desk drawer and locked it, thus surrendering himself and his country to the Fascists.

Now it became necessary to inform the authorities throughout Italy that the martial law decree publicized only hours earlier had been revoked. The telegrams countermanding the decree created widespread chaos and confusion, except among the Fascists. Now that they could be certain that the Italian army wasn't going to be an obstacle to their March, they were delighted and relieved. As they tore the decree off the walls, they cheered "King Emmanuel, the Fascist King." When the news of the king's refusal to sign the decree reached General De Bono in Perugia, he told his comrades, "It's going to be a play with a happy ending."

Actions of a Fox

The Fascist marchers were in a happy mood as they began to move toward Rome. And no wonder. What they had feared would develop into a bloody encounter had now become nothing more than a Blackshirt demonstration. The Fascists traveled on foot, in trains (for which they received free passes), and by automobile. They carried black banners and signs reading "I Don't Give a Damn" and "Rome or Death." Only a fraction of the total Fascist membership had been willing to risk their personal safety in a military expedition against Rome, but now that opposition from the army or police was unlikely, thousands of other members rushed to join the March.

Men abandoned their jobs, put on black shirts, and armed themselves with anything they could find—old pistols and muskets, garden hoes, scythes, daggers, clubs, and even sticks of dynamite. One enthusiastic Fascist who left his job was asked by his employer how long he would be away. "How do I know?" he replied. "This is a revolution!" His excitement was shared by many of the marchers as they streamed toward Rome. "Viva Mussolini," they shouted.

The Fascist mood had been different that morning, particularly in Milan. The prefect there had summoned Mussolini and placed him under arrest. For a few hours his Blackshirt entourage panicked, believing that with their Duce in jail their cause was lost. But shortly before noon came the news that the king had refused to sign the martial law decree, and Mussolini was promptly released. He and his followers were jubilant. Now that he was certain the king was for him, Mussolini became cocky with self-confidence and fully determined to hold out for everything he wanted.

Up to this point he had vacillated from the stance of a moderate to that of an extremist, sometimes agreeing with Grandi and De Vecchi that a political compromise was possible, sometimes with Balbo and Bianchi who insisted that a military expedition against Rome was the only means of winning as much power as the Fascists wanted. He could never commit himself to either of these points of view, but by favoring one and then the other, he could offer the government the hope of compromise or the threat of civil war. In the shrewd political game that he played, the March on Rome became nothing more than a military bluff, a strategic device for achieving the single objective that obsessed him: the seizure of power. Commenting on Mussolini's actions during this crisis, an Italian historian observed: "His dreams are of a lion, his actions of a fox."

On the same day that the martial law decree was revoked, De Vecchi, who had just had an audience with the king, telephoned to urge Mussolini to come to Rome. Mussolini replied that only if the king called him for consultation would he leave Milan. A little later the king's adjutant telephoned to inform him that the king wished to see him. Sensing the strength of his position, Mussolini carried his strategy one step further and told the adjutant that only if the king asked him to head the government would he agree to come to Rome.

His strategy worked. There was another telephone call conveying

Mussolini organizing the March in Milan.

a message from the king. This time Mussolini was being invited to Rome for the purpose of forming his own cabinet. But Mussolini, fearing a trick, said, "It sounds like a trap. I want an official cable." Grandi got on the phone to assure him that the message was a genuine one, but Mussolini insisted on having it in writing. He promised to fly to Rome as soon as he received it.

The telegram from the king was exactly what Mussolini wanted: "His Majesty the King begs you to proceed to Rome as soon as possible as he wishes to entrust you with the responsibility of forming a cabinet."

Mussolini's Triumph

Instead of flying to Rome, as he said he would, Mussolini decided to travel by *wagon-lit* (sleeper) on the night train. The clothes he chose for the journey may have puzzled some of his followers: a morning coat, black trousers, a bowler hat, and white spats. This formal outfit hardly seemed appropriate for one who claimed to be a revolutionist and a man of the people. But Mussolini had his own reason for wearing such a garb. It was his way of reassuring the industrialists and the other wealthy Italians who had financed his climb to power that, although he talked and wrote like a champion of the people, he knew who his most powerful friends were. After he had met with the king at the Palazzo del Quirinale in Rome, he donned the black uniform of a Fascist. The date was October 30, 1922.

That afternoon the Blackshirt marchers, whose original number of 8,000 had now swelled to more than 25,000, put on their big show. For five hours they marched past the balcony of the king's palace, shouting their slogans. On the balcony next to the king and his family was their Duce, his arm raised to them in the Roman salute adopted by the Fascists, the same salute that had been revived at Fiume by D'Annunzio.

From all parts of Italy there poured in congratulations and offers of support. These came both from Fascist sympathizers and from former anti-Fascists. The fear of what might happen to them once Mussolini took charge of the government led many an anti-Fascist to declare his allegiance to Mussolini. Among these were some of the leaders of the Disabled Soldiers' Association, who had planned to disrupt the Fascist March on Rome with a demonstration of their members led by D'Annunzio. On the same day that the Blackshirts converged on Rome, the association issued a proclamation praising the Duce. "A great hour is striking for Italy," it read in part. "We have forseen it, and have prepared for it."

The Fascist dictatorship did not come at once. At first, Mussolini seemed intent on lulling the nation into a state of security. Although he gloated over his triumph in his first speech to the Chamber of Deputies, telling them that he could, if he wished, "turn the place into an armed camp of Blackshirts" and "nail up the doors of Parliament," he behaved like the legitimate premier of a legitimate government. He punished some of his Fascist goons for their acts of violence, and he selected a cabinet which included representatives of most of the nation's principal political parties and only four Fascists.

Yet after a few months it became increasingly apparent that a police state was Mussolini's ultimate goal. He not only formed a Grand Council of Fascists which, meeting in secret, eventually supplanted the regular cabinet, but he also established his own Fascist army, at government expense, known as "The Voluntary Militia for National Security." In a false gesture of good will, he dissolved the notorious Fascist squads; but promptly absorbed many of them within his newly formed Militia. Both the Grand Council and the Militia, though illegal, became accepted elements within the new government, despite the protests of anti-Fascists.

Mussolini with his Fascist supporters, including De Bono on his right (gesturing) and De Vecchi on his left, at the conclusion of the March.

*Above: Fascists rallying in Rome
at the conclusion of the March.
Right: a crowd of citizens at a
Fascist rally in the Campidoglio in Rome.*

*Mussolini presiding over a meeting
of the ministers of his government.*

Throughout Italy, organized gangs of Fascists continued to punish and terrorize their opponents. When Giacomo Matteotti, a prominent socialist deputy, bitterly criticized the actions of Mussolini, he was murdered. Other deputies were imprisoned or driven into exile. The press was regimented. By 1928 all vestiges of Italy's democratic form of government were eliminated. The Parliament was abolished, and Mussolini became dictator of Italy in the fullest sense of the word.

His dictatorship, which Adolf Hitler was to imitate in a few years, remained in power until 1943 when it was finally crushed in the course of World War II.

Chronology

1883
JULY 29   Benito Mussolini is born in the village of Predappio, in east-central Italy

1902   Moves to Switzerland, thus avoiding military service

1903   Launches career as left-wing journalist and orator

1904   Returns to Italy to serve in army after King Victor Emmanuel III declares amnesty for draft dodgers

1909   Assumes editorship of *L'Avvenire* in Trento, Austria, but is frequently jailed and finally expelled for left-wing writings

1911   Leads two-day antiwar revolt in Forlì, and goes to jail

1912   Elected to Socialist Party executive committee, and to directorship of *Avanti,* the party's official newspaper

1914
JULY 28   Outbreak of World War I
OCTOBER   Mussolini forced to resign as director of *Avanti* after reversing his antiwar stand
NOVEMBER   Mussolini becomes editor of new newspaper, *Il Popolo D'Italia,* which favors Italy's intervention in the war

1915
MAY 24   Italy enters World War I by declaring war on Austria
SEPTEMBER 2   Mussolini reenters the army as a draftee and serves for 17 months

1918
NOVEMBER 11   World War I ends in an Armistice

1919
MARCH 23   Mussolini organizes the first Fascist contingent
SEPTEMBER   Gabriel D'Annunzio and a force of Italian ex-
            soldiers seize the city of Fiume, in defiance of the
            Versailles Treaty

1919–1920   Period of widespread unemployment and postwar
            disillusion; seizure of factories by Italian workers

1921
MAY   35 Fascists, including Mussolini, are elected to
            Italian Parliament
NOVEMBER   Mussolini convenes congress of Blackshirts for
            official founding of the Fascist Party

1922
FEBRUARY   Luigi Facta becomes prime minister of Italy
AUGUST   General strike called by socialists to protest nation-
            wide Fascist violence is a failure
OCTOBER 3   Establishment of Fascist Militia
OCTOBER 24 Fascists threaten seizure of government at giant
            rally in Naples, and secretly choose date for March
            on Rome
OCTOBER 26 Fascists begin mobilizing for the March
OCTOBER 27 Attempts to negotiate with Mussolini for a coalition
            government are unsuccessful
OCTOBER 28 The Italian cabinet imposes martial law on the na-
            tion and orders the arrest of Fascist leaders
OCTOBER 29 King Victor Emmanuel revokes the cabinet's decree
            by refusing to sign it, and summons Mussolini to
            Rome to head a new cabinet
OCTOBER 30 Mussolini arrives from Milan in a Pullman-type
            train as the Fascist marchers enter Rome

A Note on
Further Reading

There are a number of excellent biographies of Benito Mussolini which describe his background and the historical events that led to his dictatorship of Italy. The author of this volume found the following especially useful:

Borgese, G. A., *Goliath: The March of Fascism.* Viking Press, 1937.

Collier, Richard, *Duce: A Biography of Benito Mussolini.* Viking Press, 1971.

Fermi, Laura, *Mussolini.* University of Chicago Press, 1961.

Hibbert, Christopher, *Il Duce: The Life of Benito Mussolini.* Little Brown, 1962.

Seldes, George, *Sawdust Caesar.* Harper & Bros., 1935.

The author is also indebted to books by two men who were deputies in the Italian Parliament when the Fascists were coming into power: Gaetano Salvemini's *The Fascist Dictatorship in Italy* (Holt, 1927) and Emilio Lussu's *Road to Exile: The Story of a Sardinian Patriot* (Covici Friede, 1936). Salvemini was driven into exile and became a distinguished professor of history at Harvard; Lussu was imprisoned by the Fascists, but managed to escape to the United States. The two men returned to Italy after the fall of Fascism.

For those who can read Italian the author recommends Paolo Alatri's *Le Origini Del Fascismo* (Editori Riuniti, 1956), one of the best books on the origins of Italian Fascism; and Sergio Zavoli's *Nascita Di Una Dittatura* (Societa Editrice Internazionale, 1973), which is largely based on recent interviews with Italians who were participants in the historical episodes that ushered in the Fascist era. Also illuminating is the diary of Dino Grandi, a close associate of Mussolini, which deals specifically with the events surrounding the March on Rome. The diary was published in the Italian magazine *Epoca,* in October, 1972, fifty years after the March took place.

Index

The Author

Jerre Mangione was born in Rochester, New York, of Sicilian immigrant parents. He is a graduate of Syracuse University, has served on the editorial staff of *Time* and was national coordinating editor of the Federal Writers' Project. Mr. Mangione is professor of English Literature and head of the creative writing program at the University of Pennsylvania. He is the author of nine books, among them *The Dream and the Deal, A Passion for Sicilians: The World Around Danilo Dolci, America Is Also Italian,* and *Mount Allegro.*